Kuwi's Kitchen

KIWI KIDS' COOKBOOK

KAT MEREWETHER

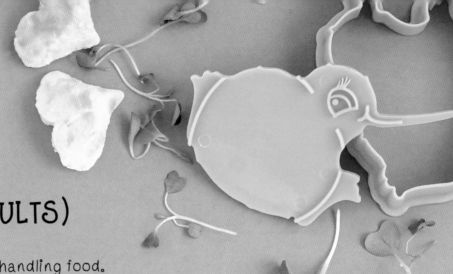

FOR THE KIDS (and ADULTS)

▶ Wash and dry your hands before handling food.

▶ Ask a grown-up before preparing food, and have them with you around heat, electronic appliances and sharp knives.

▶ Compost bins and worm farms are a great way to dispose of fruit and vege scraps, and are perfect for helping to grow awesome vegetables at home too.

▶ Check with your school or kindy about their allergy policy before taking lunchbox items containing peanut butter. If you have an allergy to an ingredient, a grown-up can help find the best alternative for you.

▶ Look for this flag to see which foods are treat foods. ← **THIS IS A** *sometimes* **TREAT FOOD**

▶ Have fun and make up your own variations. Add fruit and vegetables in creative ways to invent something new.

HAVE FUN, TRY NEW THINGS + GET CREATIVE!

FOR THE ADULTS

Part of the inspiration for this book came while searching the shelves of my local bookshop for a Kiwi cookbook for my own kids. I wanted something that would help them to practice preparing and cooking food, and to encourage them to enjoy more whole foods, and less of the processed stuff. Also, many of you have shared photos of foods that have been created with your kids, inspired by the 'Kuwi's Huhu Hunt' book, with stories about how they have helped your children to enjoy their vegetables!

I am not a chef, a medical professional or a nutritionist. This book is not about the right or wrong way to feed your children, and comes from a place of solidarity, support and non-judgement.

Guidance from a grown-up ensures kids learn safe practices, but also gives an opportunity to learn and build valuable life skills. You are welcome to adapt the recipes to suit your family, cultural, or special dietary needs. I would love to hear how you made the recipes work better for you.

Recreate, share and enjoy!

Kat M

INGREDIENT NOTES

NUTS - A few of the recipes have peanut butter in them. Please be aware that some kindergartens and schools are nut free due to allergies. Almond or sesame butter could be alternative options, but it is always best to check, as some children could have allergies to those as well.

When purchasing peanut butter, remember to read the ingredients. Try to avoid peanut butter with added fats, sugars or salt.

GLUTEN - Most of us with gluten intolerance have learned which flours make good substitutes. If the recipe is gluten free, I have added the GF symbol. However, most recipes can be made gluten free by using trusted GF ingredients. My favourite gluten free flours are made from buckwheat, chickpea, and rice. There are also some great gluten free baking mixes.

If using the recipes with rolled oats, make sure they are wheat free organic oats. However, these are not gluten free and should not be eaten by people with coeliac disease or a high sensitivity to gluten.

EGGS - Consider choosing accredited free-range eggs. If you are vegan, or can't eat eggs, you may already have a good egg substitute. There are many egg substitutes, such as aquafaba, chia seeds or apple sauce.

CHOC CHIPS - I prefer dark choc chips. If you are vegan or dairy free, check the ingredients, as often dark choc chips will suit your requirements.

YOGHURT - I love plain unsweetened yoghurt and I sometimes add blended berries, honey or a little organic jam to sweeten. Many of the sweetened store-bought flavoured yoghurts have as much added sugar as a soft drink! Plain coconut yoghurt is a great dairy free and vegan option.

SWEETNESS - I like to use Mānuka honey because of its healing properties, but any other honey is fine.

I also recommend REAL maple syrup (not maple-flavoured syrup). Real maple syrup comes from the sap of the maple tree, while maple-flavoured syrup is sugar syrup with artificial maple flavouring. Rice malt syrup is also an option.

While slightly more tasty and healthy than many refined-sugars, naturally occurring sugars should still be used in moderation.

I have one or two recipes that use brown sugar or golden syrup. This is a good indication that it is a 'sometimes' treat food.

100S & 1000S/SPRINKLES - Sometimes I use small amounts of 100s & 1000s or sprinkles to make food look more appealing to young children. Some 100s & 1000s/sprinkles contain gluten, so if you are baking gluten free, be sure to check the ingredients.

MEASUREMENTS

1 cup = 250ml

1/2 cup = 125ml

1 Tbs = 15ml

1/2 Tbs = 7.5ml

1 tsp = 5ml

1/2 tsp = 2.5ml

DIETARY ICONS

(GF) - Gluten Free

(DF) - Dairy Free

(EF) - Egg Free

(RSF) - Refined Sugar Free

🥜 - Contains Peanuts

THIS IS A *sometimes* TREAT FOOD

PLASTIC-FREE STRAWS ARE THE BEST CHOICE, OR NO STRAWS AT ALL!

CRITTER EYES (GF) (DF)

1 egg white
1/2 teaspoon lemon juice
1 1/2 cups gluten free icing sugar
Bag of dairy free dark choc chips

1. Line a baking tray with baking paper.

2. Separate the yolk and white of an egg and set the yolk aside for another recipe.

3. Lightly whisk egg white and lemon juice in a bowl.

4. Sift icing sugar and gradually add to the egg white and lemon mix, whisking until smooth and combined.

5. Place icing into a small zip-lock bag and seal.

6. With scissors, snip a very small piece off the bottom corner of the bag.

7. Using the bag, pipe the eyes onto the baking paper, each one about the size of a pea (smaller if you want tiny eyes).

8. Straight after piping the eyes, place the dark choc chips into the centre of eye, flat end down. If you are making tiny eyes, use chia seeds or black sesame seeds.

IMPORTANT: Leave to set for 24 hours.

... BECAUSE CRITTER EYES MAKE EVERYTHING MORE FUN!

CACAO NUT SMOOTHIE
Makes 2

BLEND:

2 cups almond milk*

1 banana

1 Tbs peanut butter

1 tsp cacao powder

(GF) (RSF) (EF) (DF)

PINK BERRY BANANA
Makes 2

BLEND:

1 1/2 cups almond milk*

1/2 cup coconut yoghurt

1/2 cup frozen raspberries

1 banana

1 tsp maple syrup (or honey)

(GF) (RSF) (EF) (DF)

*Always choose
unsweetened
almond milk

DELICIOUS

NUTRITIOUS

BREKKY

14

FRENCH TOAST HUHU GRUBS

4 slices sandwich bread
1 banana (quartered - sliced lengthwise & then in half)
1 egg
2 Tbs milk (or almond milk)
Pinch of cinnamon (optional)
Butter or coconut oil, to grease the pan

1. Cut crusts off the bread and flatten each slice of bread with your hands.

2. Place 1/4 of a banana on the end of a slice of bread and roll it up. Repeat until they are all filled and rolled up.

3. In a bowl, whisk the egg, milk and cinnamon.

4. Place pan over a medium heat. Add a little butter or oil.

5. Dip the rolls in the egg mix until coated. Place rolls in the pan, they will stay together better if you place them join side down.

6. Turn the rolls to cook on all sides, until golden brown.

Serve with berries, yoghurt or cacao choc (see page 63).

BREKKY MOUSSE (GF) (RSF) (EF) (DF)

Makes 2

1 cup almond milk
1/4 cup chia seeds
1 1/2 Tbs cacao powder
1/2 tsp ground cinnamon (optional)
3 drops vanilla extract
1-2 Tbs maple syrup (or honey)

1. Blend all ingredients until smooth and creamy.

2. Pop in the fridge overnight.

3. Serve chilled with fruit of your choice (bananas, mango, fresh, frozen or freeze-dried berries, kiwifruit), and coconut yoghurt.

CHOC FOR BREKKY!

TO BE MADE THE
NIGHT BEFORE

CHIA KIWI PUDDING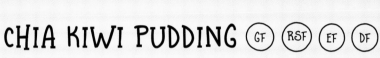

Makes 2

1 cup coconut milk
1/4 cup chia seeds
3 drops vanilla extract
2 tsp maple syrup (or honey)
1 kiwifruit

1. Add all ingredients (except kiwifruit) to a mixing bowl and whisk
   vigorously to combine. Stick 3-4 kiwifruit slices to the inside of
   the glass. Fill glass with the mixture.

2. Pop in the fridge overnight.

3. Serve topped with kiwifruit chunks.

Other topping ideas: frozen, fresh or freeze-dried raspberries,
blueberries, bananas, mango, grapefruit, pineapple and seeds.
I find the more tangy and tasty the fruit, the better!

17

DF KUWI'S FIRST EGG with TOAST

1 piece of toast bread
Coconut oil (or butter)
1 egg

1. Heat the pan to a medium heat.

2. Use your Kuwi cutter to cut out the centre of the bread.
   Stamp the cut out bread with the Kuwi cutter inner.

3. Put a little coconut oil (or butter) into the pan and pop
   in your bread, including the inner Kuwi bread.

4. Crack your egg into the centre of the outer bread.

5. Pop a lid on your pan. Cook for around 3 minutes if
   you like your egg runny, or 4-5 minutes if you like your
   eggs well done.

You could serve this resting on a bed of baby
spinach, and dip your Kuwi into the egg yolk. Yum!

TIP:
If you can't eat
eggs, you could use
the Kuwi cutter with
halloumi cheese or tofu.
Simply place the cut out
halloumi or tofu in the
centre of the bread &
cook for 2 minutes on
each side.

BREKKY BANANA BEAKS (GF) (RSF) (EF)

Can be made dairy free.

2 bananas (makes 4 banana beaks)
1/2 cup of plain yoghurt (or coconut yoghurt)
4 iceblock sticks (or you can use 4 teaspoon handles)

TOPPING IDEAS: Puffed rice, coconut, chia seeds, freeze-dried raspberries (crumbled), just a little dark choc or cacao choc (see page 63).

1. Pop your chosen toppings into a shallow dessert plate. Pour yoghurt into a tall, skinny cup.

2. Cut a peeled banana in half. Insert an iceblock stick into each piece of banana.

3. Dip each banana into the yoghurt until fully coated.

4. Carefully roll into the topping mix, or sprinkle until covered.

5. Place on a plate covered in baking paper and pop in freezer for at least 40 minutes.

APPLE OATIES

1 apple
Peanut butter
Wheat free rolled oats
Cacao choc (see page 63)

1. Cut your apple into slices.

2. Spread peanut butter onto slices and sprinkle the oats on top.

3. Drizzle a teaspoon of warm cacao across the apple oaties.

(RSF) (EF) (DF)

YOU COULD ADD YOUR CRITTER EYES BEFORE FREEZING

21

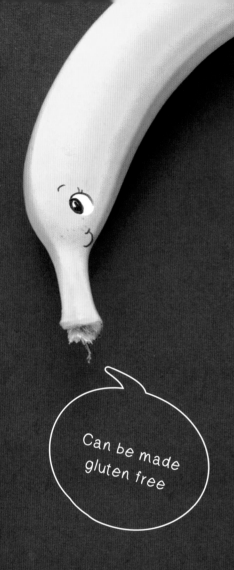

MINI BANANA PANCAKES

1/2 cup wheat free rolled oats (or buckwheat flour)
1/2 tsp baking powder
Pinch of cinnamon
1 banana
2 large eggs (or egg substitute)

1. Pop the rolled oats, baking powder and cinnamon in the food processor. Whizz on high for 2 minutes, or until it reaches a flour-like consistency.

2. Mash the banana with a fork.

3. Whisk the eggs.

4. Mix everything together.

5. Preheat the pan over a medium heat.

6. Add a little coconut oil (or butter) and pour on roughly 2 tablespoons of the mix per pancake.

7. Cook one side until lightly browned when you lift the corner.

8. Flip the pancakes. Cook for another minute or until the other side is also nicely browned.

Serve with slices of banana, berries or a squeeze of lemon juice.

Can be made gluten free

22

YOU COULD ADD A DRIZZLE OF YOGHURT, MAPLE SYRUP OR HONEY

24

KŪMARA HASH BROWNS

1 large sized kūmara (cut in half)
1 medium-sized potato
1 egg yolk (or 2 Tbs of oil, if egg free)
1/2 cup grated cheese
1/2 brown onion, finely diced
1 garlic clove crushed
1 cup breadcrumbs (or GF breadcrumbs)
1/4 cup diced fresh herbs (can use basil or parsley)

Can be made gluten free

1. Preheat oven to 220°C, or 200°C if fan-forced.

2. Place kūmara and potato on an oven tray. Cook for 45 minutes (or until flesh is soft).

3. Take out of the oven and let them cool for around 30 minutes.

4. Gently slice open the kūmara and potato and scoop out the insides.

5. Pop the kūmara and potato insides into a mixing bowl.

6. Add egg yolk, cheese, onion, garlic, breadcrumbs and herbs.

7. Mix with a fork (and mash if needed) until you have a mixture that can be moulded with your hands.

8. Place some baking paper onto an oven tray. Grease the baking paper with a little bit of oil.

9. Shape into small croquette shapes, and pop onto the baking paper with about 1cm of space between each hash brown. Drizzle or spray a little oil over them.

10. Cook for 15 minutes. Carefully remove from oven and turn the hash browns over.

11. Cook for an extra 15 minutes, or until the outside is golden brown.

12. Season to taste.

Can be served with mashed avocado, tomato sauce and fresh baby spinach.

.... FOR EXTRA GOODNESS, ADD MORE CHOPPED VEGETABLES ....

EGG MUFFIN TOPS (GF) (RSF)

6 eggs
1 cup of chopped spinach
1/2 cup of grated cheese

1. Preheat the oven to 200°C, or 180°C if fan-forced.

2. Grease 6 cups of a muffin tin with oil, or line with baking paper.

3. Crack eggs into a medium sized bowl and whisk until smooth.

4. Stir the spinach and cheese into the egg mixture.

5. Pour or spoon the egg mixture evenly into the 6 cups of the muffin tray.

6. Bake for 18 minutes or until eggs are cooked.

Serve straight away or let cool and refrigerate.

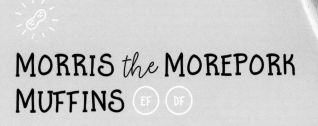

MORRIS *the* MOREPORK
MUFFINS (EF) (DF)

English muffins (or thick toast cut into circles)
Peanut or almond butter
Banana
Blueberries (or dairy free dark choc chips)
Strawberries (optional)

1. Pop your English muffins in the toaster.

2. Spread with nut spread.

3. Slice the banana to make the eyes, and pop on blueberries (or choc chips) as the pupils.

4. Carefully slice kiwifruit into a beak shape, and cut a strawberry into wing shaped slices.
   You can use sliced banana cut to wing shapes if you don't have strawberries.

TIP: USE YOUR KIWI
CUTTER TO MAKE INTERESTING
SANDWICHES

HUWI'S HEALTHY LUNCHBOX

Blueberries
- Boost brainpower
- Promote a healthy tummy
- Full of vitamins and minerals

THESE ARE SUPER FOODS!

Cucumbers
- 95% water, so they keep you hydrated
- Boost energy level
- Can even get rid of bad breath!

Almonds
- Promote strong bones & teeth
- Boost the immune system
- Promote healthy brain development
- Boost energy level

Grapes
- Promote strong bones
- Antibacterial properties

Carrots
- Protect your eyes
- Protect teeth and gums
- Full of vitamins and minerals

Snow peas are high in fibre and Vitamin C

Celery promotes a healthy tummy and reduces inflammation

Mandarins + Oranges are a super source of vitamins and minerals, especially Vitamin C, to help ward off colds

BE SURE TO CHECK OUT YOUR LOCAL FARMERS' MARKET FOR LOTS MORE SEASONAL FRUIT & VEGETABLES!

Bananas

- Source of fibre, vitamins and minerals
- Make you feel full for longer

Apples

- Great source of fibre (keep the skin on)
- Full of vitamins and minerals
- Make you feel fuller for longer

Strawberries are full of vitamins and minerals

Kiwifruit

- Help you to sleep better
- Helps your digestive system work well - softer poo, yay!

TIP: Cut fruit & vegetables into bite-sized pieces & interesting shapes

31

FROG EGGS (EF) (DF)

1 1/2 cups of wheat free rolled oats
1/2 Tbs cacao powder
1 ripe banana
3 Tbs maple syrup (or honey)
1 1/2 Tbs peanut butter*, almond or sesame seed butter
1/2 Tbs coconut oil
1/4 tsp vanilla extract
1 Tbs dairy free dark choc chips

1. Pop the rolled oats and cacao powder into a food processor. Whizz on high for 2-3 minutes, until it becomes flour-like.

2. Add the banana, maple syrup, nut butter, coconut oil and vanilla extract and whizz until it reaches a dough like consistency. If it is still too flaky, add small amounts of warm water, and combine until it comes together.

3. Move the mixture into a bowl, and roll the dough into bite-sized balls.

4. Add 3-4 choc chips per ball. Store in the fridge.

*ALLERGY NOTE: Check your school or kindy's allergy policy.

KUWI BITES ⊙ⒹⒻ 🥜

Follow the first two steps from the Frog Eggs recipe, on the opposite page.

EXTRAS:
Critter eyes (see page 10)
Pretzel sticks or toothpicks (for the beak)
2 Tbs cacao choc (see page 63)

3. Move the mixture into a bowl, and roll the dough into balls.

4. Press in your pre-made critter eyes and pretzel stick beaks.

5. To melt the cacao choc, pop it into a bowl and place into a shallow bowl of hot water (careful not to get water into the cacao choc). Once melted, dip the Kuwi bites into the cacao choc and pop onto baking paper to create a base.

6. Store in the fridge.

TASTY POPCORN

2 Tbs coconut oil
1/2 cup popcorn kernels (uncooked)
1/2 tsp onion powder
1/2 tsp garlic powder
1/2 tsp paprika powder
1/2 tsp ground cumin
1/2 tsp salt (I use fine rock salt)

1. Add coconut oil to a large pot (must have a lid), and place over a medium heat on the stove top.

2. Add just four popcorn kernels. Wait until they pop, remove them and add the rest of the cup of popcorn kernels.

3. Put a lid on the pot and take the pot off the element for 30 seconds.

4. Put the pot back on the element (still at a medium heat).

5. Jiggle the pot occasionally until the popping slows down.

6. Remove from heat (before popping stops).

7. After a couple of minutes, remove the lid. This will help make your popcorn crisp.

8. Place the powdered onion, garlic, paprika, cumin and salt in a bag (preferably paper or re-usable) and shake.

9. Add your popcorn and shake well until popcorn is well covered.

KIWICORN POPCORN (GF) (EF) (DF)

3 Tbs coconut oil
1 cup popcorn kernels (uncooked)
1 Tbs warm maple syrup (or honey)
1/2 tsp 100s & 1000s

Follow the Tasty Popcorn recipe
on the opposite page, to the end of
step 7.

8. Add warm maple syrup or honey and
   stir it in.

9. Place your popcorn into a bag
   (preferably paper or re-usable) and
   add the 100s & 1000s. Shake it up.

YUM SNAILS, SLUGS and BUGS

Snail 1
Celery + sliced kiwifruit + almond + cream cheese

Snail 2
Celery + sliced orange + almond + cream cheese

Snail 3*
Celery + cucumber + grape + peanut butter

Ladybug 1
Rice cracker + hummus + cherry tomatoes + olive bits

Ladybug 2
Cherry tomatoes + olives

Ladybug 3
Strawberries + cacao nibs

Moths*
1/2 crackers or pretzels (wings) + Celery + peanut butter

Caterpillars
Grapes + skewers

Make up your own crazy critter combinations!

JUST ADD CRITTER EYES!

*ALLERGY NOTE:
Check your school or
kindy's allergy policy.
You could swap
peanut butter for
hummus or
cream cheese.

MANDARIN SNAILS

1. Carefully peel your mandarin leaving a strip of peel around the outside.

2. Remove the band of peel and carefully cut out the snail shape. Add eyes using a permanent marker.

3. Place mandarin into the peel to create your snail. You could use some almond butter to hold it together.

BUTTERFLY BAGGIES

OPTIONS:
Apple slices
Grapes
Berries
Pea pods
Celery
Finely chopped or baby carrots
Seeds/nuts*

EXTRAS:
Small snap-lock bags
Sturdy wooden or plastic pegs/clips
Googly eyes & glue (can draw onto cardboard)

1. Either draw eyes onto your peg with a permanent marker, or glue the googly eyes on and allow glue to dry.

2. Place food into bag to fill the both halves of your bag equally, and to allow it to close with a bit of room in the top and centre of the bag.

3. Scrunch up the middle of the bag and clip on the peg/clip, being careful not to squish the food.

IMPORTANT: Please do not throw out your pegs or plastic bags. You can wash, dry and reuse, if they get grubby.

 *BE ALLERGY AWARE

... DON'T BE AFRAID TO MIX IT UP ...

PARSNIP CHIPS

1 parsnip
2 Tbs olive or rice bran oil
1/2 tsp fine sea/rock salt (optional)

1. Preheat oven to 220°C, or 200°C if fan-forced, and line an oven tray with baking paper.

2. Wash parsnip, cut off the top and use a vegetable peeler to make thin slices of parsnip (about the size of a potato chip).

3. In a large bowl, combine the oil, salt and parsnip slices.

4. Place the parsnip slices onto the lined oven trays.

5. Cook for 30 - 35 minutes or until browned and crisp.

6. Check after 15 minutes, as some ovens bake faster than others.

7. Once cooked, take chips out of the oven and let them air cool.

NOT-NACHOS

1 1/2 cups finely grated carrots
(packed down)
1/2 cup water
1/2 cup grated cheese
2 eggs
4 Tbs gluten free flour (or plain flour)
1/2 tsp fine sea/rock salt (optional)
1/2 tsp paprika powder (optional)

1. Preheat oven to 200°C, or 180°C if fan-forced, and line an oven tray with baking paper.

2. Mix carrots and water in a microwave safe bowl, and heat on high for 3 minutes.

3. Drain the carrots and use an old tea towel to squeeze excess water out until they are quite dry.

4. Pop carrots back in the bowl and mix in the eggs, cheese and flour.

5. Create shapes on the baking paper tray, using a bikkie cutter. They should be around 1/2 a centimetre thick.

6. Bake for 13-15 minutes or until crispy on the edges.

SERVE WITH A SIMPLE SALSA OR GUACAMOLE.

FOR THE PECKISH!

FLORENCE *the* FANTAIL MUESLI BARS (GF) (RSF) (DF) (EF)

1 cup shredded coconut
1 cup raw almonds
1 cup raw cashews
1/4 cup almond butter
1/2 Tbs maple syrup
1 Tbs honey
2 Tbs cacao choc (see page 63)
2-3 Tbs water

1. Line a baking pan with baking paper.

2. Place all ingredients except the water into a food processor. Pulse. If mixture doesn't stick together, add a tablespoon of water. Keep adding water and pulsing until the mixture comes together.

3. Place mixture into the pre-lined baking pan. Press it down until it is evenly distributed and refrigerate overnight.

4. Cut into muesli bar shapes.

5. Drizzle with cacao choc.

42

Kuwi's Glorious GRUB

HUWI'S SEED SALAD

A mix of any 3 types of leafy green lettuce
(not iceburg lettuce)
2 Tbs sunflower seeds
1 Tbs pumpkin seeds
1 Tbs extra virgin olive oil or avocado oil
1 lemon

1. Pop lettuce into a sieve or colander and rinse
   the lettuce with cold water. Set aside to drain.

2. Once drained, pop the lettuce into a bowl.

3. Sprinkle seeds over the lettuce.

4. Mix a squeeze of lemon and the oil in a cup
   and pour over salad.

AS SEEN IN 'KUWI'S HUHU HUNT'

46

HUHU GRUB BITES

200g halloumi cheese
1 sheet of flaky pastry
1 egg
20 googly eyes

1. Preheat oven to 200°C, or 180°C if fan-forced, and line a baking/oven tray with baking paper.

2. Cut the halloumi block into 10 pieces.

3. Thinly cut the sheet of pastry into 10 thin strips (about 1-1.5cm thick).

4. Roll 1 pastry strip around each piece of halloumi and place them onto the baking tray.

5. Beat an egg and add 1/2 a teaspoon of water. Brush the egg mix onto the pastry.

6. Pop in the oven for 15 minutes or until golden brown.

7. Add your critter eyes.

I like to serve these with large basil leaves or baby spinach. Wrap the Huhu Grub Bite in the leaf.

YUMMY WITH TOMATO SAUCE

47

BEST BAKED BEANS
Serves 2

1 brown onion (diced finely)
1 cup of canned tomatoes
1/2 a can of mixed beans (or butter beans,
they look more like traditional baked beans)
1/2 cup of chopped up cherry tomatoes
Pinch of rock salt

1. Heat a splash of oil in a fry pan over a
   medium heat.

2. Add diced onions and cook until they are a bit
   see-through.

3. Add the canned tomatoes and simmer for
   2-3 minutes.

4. Drain the water from the can and rinse the
   beans. Add beans and cherry tomatoes to the
   pan. Cook for a further 5 minutes.

5. Add pinch of salt to taste.

BEAN TACOS (GF)

Soft GF corn tacos
Best Baked Beans (see opposite page)
Lettuce
Cheese (optional)
Avocado (if in season)

1. Heat tacos following the instructions on the taco packaging.

2. Add to taco a heaped tablespoon of best baked beans, lettuce, a sprinkle of cheese and mashed avocado (if in season).

IF YOU LIKE SPICY FOOD, ADD A TINY DROP OF HOT SAUCE

49

AS SEEN IN 'KUWI'S HUHU HUNT'

SNAIL SUSHI

1 1/2 cups sushi rice
1 Tbs maple syrup (optional)
2 Tbs rice wine vinegar (optional)
4 seaweed sheets
2 tablespoons egg mayonnaise (optional)
1 avocado (if in season)
1 small cucumber*
1 carrot

* You can add lots more too, such as red and yellow capsicum, beetroot, and pickled ginger.

You will need a sushi mat (I got mine from a dollar store)

1. Rinse the uncooked rice in a sieve until water runs clear. Let rice drain.

2. Place rice in rice cooker with 1 1/2 cups of cold water, until cooked. If you don't have a rice cooker, place rice and 1 and a 1/2 cups cold water in a pot with a lid on it, over medium heat. Bring to the boil. Turn down to low and continue cooking for around 10 minutes, or until water is absorbed. Remove from heat, stir rice and pop the lid back on. Wait for at least 10 minutes before using.

3. Combine and microwave vinegar and maple syrup on high for 30 seconds. With a spoon, gently stir the vinegar mix into the rice.

4. On a sushi mat, place the seaweed sheet shiny side down. Evenly spread 3/4 cup of rice over the seaweed sheet, and leave about a 2cm gap at the short end.

5. Finely cut cucumber, avocado, carrot (and any other vege you choose), and place in the centre of the rice. Add a little mayonnaise. Use the sushi mat to roll into a tight sushi roll. Slightly wetting the edge like an envelope helps it to seal.

6. Cut the sushi roll into 6 pieces. Repeat until all of the seaweed sheets are used up.

SERVE WITH A LITTLE TAMARI SOY SAUCE

KUWI'S KŪMARA FRITTERS (GF) (DF) (RSF)

2 medium sized peeled kūmara (raw)
1/2 a small zucchini
2 eggs
1/2 tsp paprika powder
1/4 tsp salt
1 clove garlic crushed
1/4 onion, finely chopped.

1. Finely grate the kūmara and zucchini into a mixing bowl and stir in all other ingredients until combined.

2. Heat pan over a medium to high heat and add oil.

3. Take a heaped tablespoon of the batter and place onto pan surface. Flatten out gently into fritter shape.

4. Cook 4-5 minutes on each side, until cooked through and golden brown.

5. Repeat until all the batter is used up.

Serve with Huwi's Seed Salad (page 46).

KUWI EGGS

(GF) (DF) (RSF)

Free-range eggs
Carrots
Black olives

1. Hard boil the eggs for 8-10 minutes depending on the size of the egg.

2. Cool eggs in a bowl of cold water and then peel.

3. Carefully slice a carrot into a kiwi beak shape, and cut a slot in the egg to fit the beak.

4. Use a straw to cut out olive eyes, and then use the straw to make holes in the eggs to insert the olive eyes into.

SERVE WITH A YUMMY FRESH SALAD

54

KUWI EGG PIE

3 'ready rolled' sheets short crust pastry
10 eggs
3 tsp milk
1 small zucchini (finely grated)
1/4 cup crumbled feta cheese
1/2 onion (finely diced)

1. Preheat oven to 190°C, or 170°C if fan-forced, and grease a 20-25cm diameter pie dish.

2. Thaw 2 sheets of pastry. Use 1 sheet of pastry to line the pie dish. Let the pastry drape slightly over the sides, and trim off excess.

3. Prick the base with a fork and bake for 8 minutes.

4. Crack 9 eggs into a bowl, and leave one aside. Whisk eggs and milk together. Mix in the grated zucchini and crumbled feta.

5. Once the base has finished, remove from oven and sprinkle with the diced onion.

6. Pour egg and vege mix into the pie base.

7. Cover with the second sheet of pastry, and gently press down edges with your fingertips. Trim off excess pastry.

8. Take the third sheet of pastry out of the freezer and use Kuwi cutter and other biscuit cutters to cut out shapes and decorate the top. This is easiest when the pastry is still slightly frozen. Once the pie is decorated, use a kitchen brush and the last egg (whisked) to glaze the pastry.

9. Pop in the oven and cook for 35 minutes. Check on the pie, and put back in the oven for an extra 10 minutes, or until cooked through. You can cover with tinfoil if it's already looking nice and golden on top, to avoid it burning.

SLOW-COOKER MOTH MACARONI (RSF) (EF)

1 1/2 cups of dry macaroni elbows
1 1/2 cups of tasty cheese, grated
4 cups milk
1 head of fresh broccoli or cauliflower (or a mix of both)
1/2 tsp cornflour
Fresh basil leaves (optional)

1. Pop dry macaroni, cheese and milk in the slow cooker, mix through and set the slow cooker on high for 2 hours. If possible, stir a couple of times while cooking.

2. Place the broccoli/cauliflower into the food processor and whizz for about 30 seconds. If you don't have a food processor, you can cut it up finely.

3. Add the broccoli/cauliflower and cornflour while still in the slow-cooker and give it a stir. Cook for an extra 20 minutes.

Serve with a sprinkling of grated cheese and with basil leaves as the moth wings.

NOTE: Test the pasta after an hour as different pasta may cook faster, and you don't want it too soft.

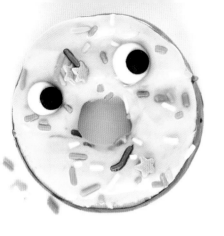

TASTY
Sweet
TREATS

A MIX OF HEALTHY EVERYDAY TREATS
& CELEBRATION 'SOMETIMES' TREAT FOODS

FEIJOA MUFFINS

4 large (or 5 medium) feijoas
1/2 cup brown sugar
1 egg
100g melted butter (or coconut oil)
1/2 cup milk (or almond milk)
1 1/2 cups of flour
1 1/2 tsp baking powder
1/2 tsp cinnamon

1. Preheat oven to 200°C, or 180°C if fan-forced, and grease a muffin tray.

2. Wash feijoas, remove the top and chop them up (skin and all). Pop the feijoas into a bowl and gently stir in the brown sugar, egg, melted butter and milk.

3. Sift flour, baking powder and cinnamon into the wet mix, and gently combine. If you over mix, they can get a bit tough.

4. Spoon mixture evenly into the muffin tray.

5. Cook for 18-20 min, or until cooked through.

THIS IS A
sometimes
TREAT FOOD

CACAO MUD POOLS

Cut fruit of your choice into slices and serve with skewers and the melted cacao choc for a delicious fruit fondue.

POUR INTO SHAPED ICE CUBE TRAYS AND FREEZE TO MAKE CHOC PIECES

CACAO CHOC (GF) (RSF) (EF) (DF)

1/2 cup cacao butter (finely grated)
1/2 cup organic coconut oil
6 Tbs organic cacao powder
3 Tbs maple syrup for sweetening (optional)
(Never microwave any of the ingredients)

1. Melt the grated cacao butter and coconut oil by putting it in a bowl and placing that into a large bowl of shallow, hot (not boiling) water. Do not allow any water to get into the cacao butter and coconut oil.

2. Once it is melted, add the maple syrup and stir to combine.

3. Add the cacao powder and mix well. Once it is melted, combined and smooth, remove from the warm water bath.

4. For a runny mix, keep warm. For solid choc, pop in fridge. You can also make into moulds and keep in the fridge.

YOGHURT FRUIT DIP

In a small bowl, mix plain yoghurt, 1/2 a teaspoon of honey, and a sprinkling of fresh or freeze-dried raspberries.

(GF) (RSF) (EF)

For a 'shiny bum' version, push a jaffa into the dough before cooking.

64

KUWI BIKKIES

2 cups plain flour
1/2 tsp baking soda
1 Tbs ground ginger
1 cup soft brown sugar
150g butter (cubed)
1 egg (beaten)
1 Tbs golden syrup

YOU CAN ADD JAFFAS

1. Preheat oven to 180°C bake, or 160°C if fan-forced. Line two baking trays with baking paper.

2. Mix flour, baking soda, ginger and sugar in a bowl. Add the butter and rub in with your hands until combined. Add the beaten egg and golden syrup and stir.

3. If the dough is too wet/sticky, add a small amounts of flour until the dough is workable.

4. Wrap in plastic wrap and refrigerate for 1 hour (or more).

5. Place on a well-floured surface and roll out until about 1/2 a centimetre thick.

6. Cut out shapes using Kuwi biscuit cutters and place on trays. The easiest way to use the cutter is with the insert in, push the outside down and then press the insert down last. Then pick up the cutter with the dough still inside, and place on the baking paper by pushing out the insert. Take extra care with Kuwi's beak.

7. Bake for 7-8 minutes until golden brown. Cool on a wire rack.

THIS IS A
sometimes
TREAT FOOD

KIWICORN POO (GF) (EF)

1 cup of plain yoghurt
2 Tbs berry jam
1/2 tsp maple syrup or honey

1. Line a baking tray with baking paper.

2. Mix berry jam and maple syrup into the cup of yoghurt.
   For different colours, use different coloured jams or
   a drop of natural food colouring.

3. Place yoghurt into a small zip-lock bag
   and close the bag. With scissors, snip a
   very small piece off the bottom corner
   of the bag.

4. Using the bag, pipe the yoghurt onto
   the baking paper, so each one is
   roughly the size of a 10c coin.

5. Freeze overnight. Keep frozen until
   you are ready to eat, as they will
   melt into yoghurt again as they thaw.

I like to top some with a few sprinkles
for a bit of Kiwicorn magic!

GF HEALTHY APPLE DONUTS

2 apples
1/2 cup plain yoghurt
1 Tbs berry jam
1 tsp maple syrup (or honey)
1/2 tsp 100s & 1000s or sprinkles
Natural food colouring (optional - to get the desired colours)

1. Carefully cut an apple so that the core is in the centre of the apple slice. Cut the core out carefully to leave a circle hole.

2. Mix yoghurt, jam and honey and add a tiny drop of food colouring.

3. Spread yoghurt onto the cut apples, sprinkle with 100s & 1000s and serve.

KUWI APPLE PUFFS (RSF)

Makes 6

2 sheets of 'ready rolled' flat puff pastry
(or 1 of flat puff pastry & 1 of flat short pastry)
2 apples (peeled and cut into thin slices)
1 egg (beaten)
Cinnamon
Honey (or maple syrup)

1. Preheat oven to 200°C, or 180°C if fan-forced, and line 2 baking/oven trays with baking paper.

2. Take 1 sheet of short (or puff) pastry out of the freezer and let it sit for only a minute. Cut out 6 Kuwi shapes with your Kuwi cutter and insert stamp, and place them carefully onto one of the trays lined with baking paper. Pop them in the freezer.

3. With the leftover scraps, cut out shapes with a small cookie cutter (optional). Pop them in the freezer with the Kuwi cut outs.

4. Thaw out the sheet of flaky pastry. Carefully slice into 6 even rectangles and pop onto the baking tray.

5. Place the apple slices in the centre of the pastry (see photo), leaving around 1-2 centimetres of edges showing. Sprinkle the apple pieces with a pinch (or more) of cinnamon and a good drizzle of honey.

6. Add your 'Kuwi' cut outs straight from the freezer to the top of the apples and brush the egg mix onto the top of all of the visible pastry.

7. Bake in the centre of the oven for 20-25 minutes, or until golden.

TIP: Cut outs keep their shape better with short pastry

69

KIWICORN BEAKS
with BANANA ICE CREAM

1 cup plain yoghurt
2 Tbs berry jam
1 tsp maple syrup or honey
2 tsp 100s & 1000s or sprinkles
4 ice cream cones
3 bananas (peeled)

KIWICORN BEAKS

1. Fill the cup with yoghurt, stir in jam and honey/maple syrup.

2. Set up a plate lined with baking paper. Pop the plate in the fridge and the sprinkles in a shallow bowl.

3. Take the ice cream cone and dip it top first into the yoghurt. Next, lightly scatter the sprinkles onto the yoghurt dipped cone. Place onto the plate in the freezer and repeat.

4. Freeze for at least 1/2 an hour.

BANANA ICE CREAM

1. Cut the banana into pieces and pop in an airtight container. Cover and put in the freezer for at least 2 hours.

2. Pop the bananas into the food processor and whizz until smooth, around 3-5 minutes. At first it will look flaky, but just keep blending. You will need to stop the processor and scrape the banana from the sides a few times.

3. Serve immediately, or scoop into a container and freeze.

CLASSIC KIWI FAIRY BREAD

Sandwich bread
Butter, cream cheese or dairy free spread
Jam (optional)
100s & 1000s or sprinkles

1. Spread butter, cream cheese or jam on the bread and cut into shapes.

2. Top with a sprinkling of 100s & 1000s or sprinkles.

KUWI BIKKIE CUTTER IDEAS

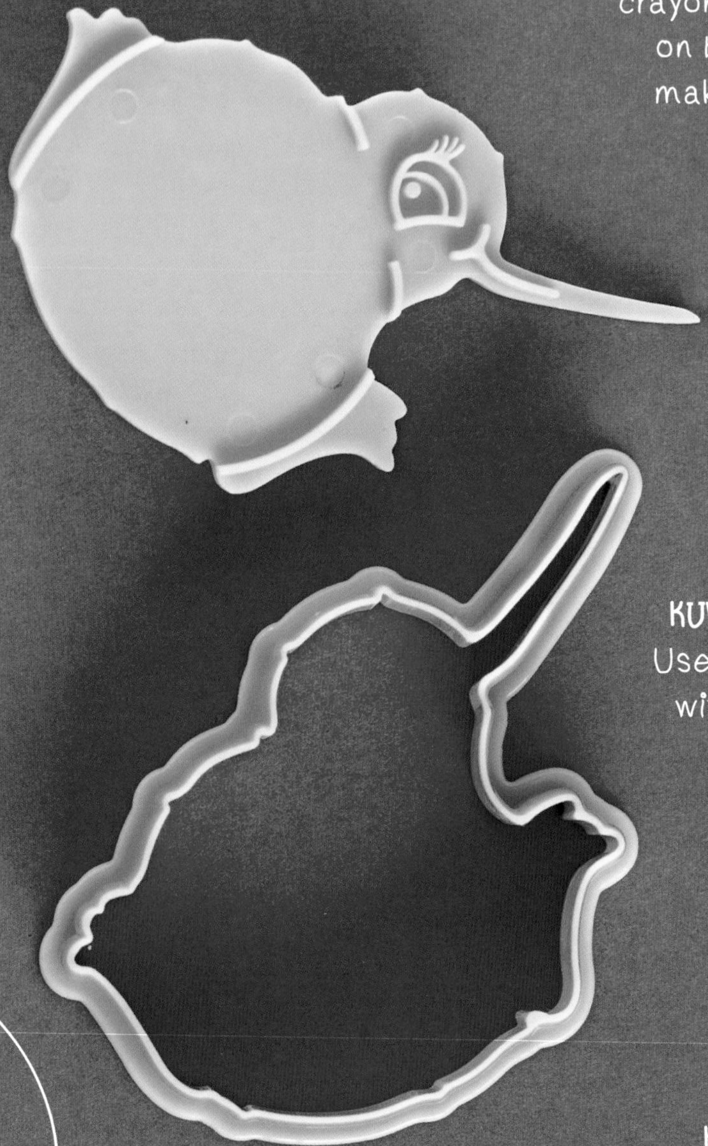

KUWI CRAYONS
Melt old crayons.
Carefully pour melted
crayons into Kuwi cutter
on baking paper, to
make new crayons!

KUWI CAKE
For special occasions,
make your own Kuwi
cake topper using
fondant icing.

KUWI PLAY DOUGH
Use the Kuwi cutter
with home-made
play dough.

KUWI TATTOO
Use a non-toxic stamp
pad, and press Kuwi
cutter on to ink both the
outer shell, and the inner
design. Press on skin.

KUWI BIKKIES
Decorate the Kuwi Bikkie
recipe with different
coloured royal icing.

KUWI FRUIT

Slice pineapple and watermelon and use the Kuwi cutter to cut out fruity Kuwi shapes.

KUWI CHRISTMAS DECORATIONS

Use polymer clay. Knead until soft, roll out and use Kuwi cutter on it. Use a toothpick to pop a hole in the top so you can hang it after cooking. Follow the cooking instructions on the packet.

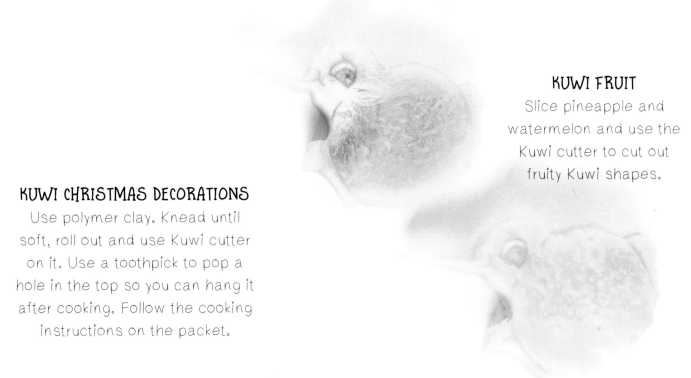

GET CREATIVE & MAKE YOUR OWN KUWI GIFTS!

A BIG THANKS TO:

Kam, for his 'Best Baked Beans' recipe. Alex, for his secret 'Cacao Choc' recipe. Walton Street Cafe/Carl, for the kitchen. Georgia and Chelsea, for making sure there was no waste (by eating all the food). Jayde, for running up and down the stairs countless times to shoot the food as we made it, and doing such a gorgeous job of capturing it. Laura, for the laughs while editing the book.

Also, thanks to all of the grown-ups and kids who have shared photos of their creations, inspired by the 'Kuwi's Huhu Hunt' book. You helped to spark the idea, and influence the content of this book!

Food Prep: Kam Chadderton

Photography: Jayde Krippner

Food Prep: Kyle Merewether

Food critics: Willow & Florence

A LITTLE BIT ABOUT KAT

Kat Merewether is an author, illustrator, and designer based in rural Te Awamutu. She spent her childhood exploring the slopes of Mount Pirongia. As she grew, so did her passion for conservation and her talent for art.

Kat's dream of becoming a children's book author and illustrator came to fruition with her Kuwi the Kiwi™ series. *Kuwi's First Egg* landed in the NZ overall top ten bestsellers list for 2015, and *Kuwi's Very Shiny Bum* was in the overall top ten for 2016. Two of her Kuwi titles were shortlisted for the 2016 New Zealand Book Awards for Children and Young Adults, with *Te Hua Tuatahi a Kuwi* winning the Children's Choice – Te Reo Māori Award.

Kat donates a portion of every book sale to Kiwis for kiwi. Through this initiative, more than 100 kiwi chicks have been supported by the series, through the Operation Nest Egg programme. She also travels the country talking to children about kiwi conservation, in her role as an official Kiwis for kiwi ambassador.

Having three daughters of her own, Kat understands what it is like to have picky eaters. She hopes that this cookbook will help to inspire households to get creative with their meals and encourage fussy eaters to try new foods.

HOW KIWIS FOR KIWI ARE SAVING KIWI

The work being done to save kiwi has many facets, involves many people, and is under way from the top of the North to the tip of the South Island, and on many offshore islands.

Some work is hands-on and operational—perhaps building a predator-proof fence or setting traps to kiwi predators. Other work may be research in the field to learn more about kiwi behaviour or research in the laboratory to find out more about kiwi genetics.

A LITTLE BIT ABOUT KIWI

- An average of 20 kiwi are killed by predators EVERY WEEK. That's a population decline of around 1,000 kiwi every year (almost 2%). At this rate, kiwi may disappear from the mainland in our lifetime.
- A single roaming dog can wipe out an entire kiwi population in a matter of days.
- In areas under where predators are controlled, 50-60% of chicks survive. When areas are not under management 95% of kiwi die before reaching breeding age.
- Only a 20% survival rate of kiwi chicks is needed for the population to increase.

KUWIS VERY SHINY BUM

KUWIS HUHU HUNT

KUWIS FIRST EGG

Some work takes precious eggs and chicks from the wild, and nurtures them in safe places until they can better protect themselves from stoats and other predators.

We also train dogs to avoid kiwi. Much of the work that is done is by communities, iwi and hapū, who together protect hundreds of thousands of hectares so that kiwi can survive and flourish.

For more info, visit **www.kiwisforkiwi.org**

The five formally described kiwi species are:

Little spotted kiwi (A. owenii) on several offshore islands & at Karori Sanctuary in Wellington & Cape Kidnappers in Hawke's Bay

Great spotted kiwi/roroa (A. haastii) in the northern South Island

Brown kiwi (Apteryx mantelli) in the North Island

Rowi (A. rowi) at Okarito, on the West Coast of the South Island

Tokoeka (A. australis) in the South Island (Fiordland, the Haast Range & on Stewart & Kapiti Islands).

THE KUWI THE KIWI SERIES OF BOOKS DONATES A PORTION OF BOOK SALES TO KIWIS FOR KIWI. TO DATE WE HAVE DONATED OVER $10,000!

First published in 2017 by Illustrated Publishing
P.O.Box 117, Te Awamutu 3840, New Zealand, Aotearoa
Text and Illustrations © Kat Merewether, 2017
Photography by Jayde Krippner

Printed in China by an accredited ISO 14001 printer

A catalogue record for this book is available from the National
Library of New Zealand.

ISBN: 978-0-994-13643-5

Illustrated
PUBLISHING

For more about this book and other
titles, visit www.illustrated.co.nz